Stop Buying Clothes You Don't Wear

How To Find Your Signature Style For Less

Charmaine Bryan

Charmaine Bryan

Toronto, Canada

www.stopbuyingclothesyoudontwear.com

ISBN: 978-1-77277-080-3

Printed in Canada

Contents

I dedicate this book to you the reader
who wants to find your signature style for less.

Acknowledgements

I would like to thank Rosa Greco my book architect, for your support and guidance in helping me to write the book. Without your encouragement I would have procrastinated and not completed this book.

I would like to thank my family who have always encouraged me to not settle for anything but the best and supporting me in what I do. When I said I wanted to start my own business you were behind me and you cheered me on when I told you about writing this book.

Thank you to my coach Noel Walrond, who truly led me on this path to personal development, for giving me the confidence to start my business and to seek out further personal and professional development opportunities.

Many thanks to my coach and mentor, Sarah Hathorn for giving me the guidance to grow my business and providing the essential constructive feedback when necessary.

Thank you to Kathryn Mackenzie, Deborah Austin, Sarah Hathorn, Karen Aguilera, Francisca Epale, Joanne Rae, Lidvina Rajabalan, Shade Lapite, Michelle Peart and Aimee Stricker for reading my chapters.

My fellow authors, Francisca Epale, Aimee Stricker and Christopher Rose. From the moment we met in the Get Your Book Done workshop and afterwards, your words were motivating. Thank you to my tutors, colleagues and friends from my George Brown Image Consulting classes. This is where my journey to entrepreneurship started and you were right there with me. Thank you for the encouragement along the way.

To my friends around the world, thank you. You have all been my cheerleaders championing me and my work.

Praise for *Stop Buying Clothes You Don't Wear*

All readers will benefit personally and professionally from applying Charmaine's detailed advice on choosing the correct clothing. By knowing which clothes and accessories to avoid and which to buy, not only will frustration levels will be lessened since your time and money are being saved but happiness levels will rise as a result of your enhanced self-confidence. I know that as a professional speaker, who needs professional co-ordinated attire, her advice will be invaluable.

Kathryn MacKenzie M.Ed., Speaker, Coach, Author

Not ready yet to hire an image consultant? Then grab this new how-to-handbook where Charmaine shares modern strategies from A-Z on image consulting techniques. In *Stop Buying Clothes You Don't Wear*, she guides you through how to determine your authentic style, what to wear for your specific body type, looking more vibrant in wearing the perfect colors, wardrobe, shopping strategies and more... I found Charmaine's wardrobe advice worth a hundred times the cost of this book. If you are looking to elevate your professional image, this book is a must-read to have in your business toolkit!

Sarah Hathorn, AICI CIM, Illustra Consulting

Stop Buying Clothes you don't Wear: How to Find Your Signature Style for Less is a must-read for those who want to improve their image personally and professionally. The way you dress will determine how you will be addressed. This book is full of thought-provoking facts, details and examples such as style personality and clothes to fit your body type. I highly recommend this book!

Francisca Epale, Interpreter, Educator and John Maxwell Certified Trainer, Award-Winning Author of *The Naked Educator: How to Survive in the Middle Kingdom*

An entertaining and informative go-to resource for enhancing one's personal style and improving clothes shopping habits. Packed full of practical tips and insights which are invaluable for anyone looking to improve their wardrobe with the best items to enhance their body shape. This great resource also equips readers with useful knowledge on how to stretch one's shopping budget further and make the most out of any clothes shopping experience. A must read for fashion stylists and designers too.

Karen Aguilera, Fashion Designer

I met Charmaine in March 2016 I could immediately see her passion for her craft, it was unmistakable. Writing any book is a labour of love, and this one is well done and informative.

Joanne Rae, AICI CIP

As an entrepreneur, small business owner or corporate professional, the image that you project is important. You want to convey the best possible image in order for people to invest in your products and services. *Stop Buying Clothes You Don't Wear* is a wonderful book for people who want to elevate their personal style. If you are looking for tips and strategies to enhance your signature style this book will help you to achieve that goal.

Deborah Austin, DTM, Speaker, Writer, Trainer, Coach & Consultant

If you find shopping for clothes overwhelming, stressful and unpleasant, Charmaine's practical guide to creating a great wardrobe is perfect for you. As someone who barely shops for these same reasons, I found the book full of realistic tips and advice on how to improve my shopping experience in an affordable and sensible way. Charmaine really puts herself in the shoes of a person in need of help to make sure they look great, make good wardrobe decisions and do it all within a budget. Grab this book to get on the road to looking and feeling your best!

Lidvina Rajabalan, Health and Nutrition Policy Researcher

Charmaine has captured her natural sense of style, her innate understanding of what colour, shape and texture helps a person look their best; and she has shared those insights in this easy-to-follow book.

Shade Lapite, Web Editor and Journalist

This book is a must read if you are ready to honor your best self, love what you wear and what is in your closet! Charmaine's easy-to-follow suggestions and budget-saving ideas are presented in the most organized and thoughtful ways to make the task of choosing the perfect types of clothing, shoes and accessories for your lifestyle an enjoyable process! Charmaine recommends that you connect with your personality, body type, desires and feelings in order to help make wardrobe and accessory choices for each day, which is fabulous! She also describes organizing items into modules so that getting ready in the morning becomes a pleasure. As a decluttering coach, I would recommend this book and Charmaine's services to you if in the process of decluttering what is in your wardrobe and ready to commit to choosing clothing styles that make you feel and look radiant inside and out!

Aimee Stricker, Award Winning Author of *Divine Decluttering*, Decluttering & Conscious Creating Expert, Inspirational Jewelry Designer, Speech-Language Pathologist

This must read book is a roadmap to successfully defining your signature personal style for all occasions.

Michelle Peart, Finance Coordinator

Praise for Charmaine's Packages and Seminars

I had my style and colour analysis with Charmaine almost 6 months ago. She provided me excellent and extensive advice about colours and styles and about what colours look best on me and what styles to wear to suit my body type. I find it easier to pick what to wear for work and other occasions. Charmaine has helped to understand the impact of different colours and outfits. Now when I go shopping I save time and money on only styles that suit me. I have been complemented on my look since we have worked together. If you are interested in highlighting your beauty and improving your self-confidence, schedule an appointment with Charmaine. She will be a wonderful help!
Negin Vatandoost, Research and Policy Analyst

People who know me can really see the difference in me! I always though "Image Consultants" are just for rich people. I thought dressing and looking good is all about spending money. Charmaine has proved me wrong and shown me otherwise. I feel like a new person and I cannot even begin to say how many complements I get every day! How is this for an example: My husband (who tends to be a very quiet person) asked me why I was suddenly glowing and looked so hot ;). My C.E.O at work walked past my desk and came back to tell me how awesome I looked and asked me what was I doing differently. Well here is what is different - it's Charmaine! You would be amazed how much difference it makes knowing your colours and outfit style that best suit your body type. Not to mention, all of it without breaking my bank!

Tasnuva Husan, Research Officer

As a fashion designer I develop practical clothing that enhances the human form and silhouette. Charmaine's role is crucial to the next stage, putting together a whole new look which reflects on the garments, accessories and footwear being worn as well as hair and makeup. Without expert advice on how all these elements work together, key impressions and personal assets may be lost. Charmaine's skills in styling and image presentation are invaluable and sure give clients renewed confidence in themselves and their wardrobe.

Karen Aguilera, Fashion Designer

"Amazing presentation! Clear delivery and great content."

"I liked that you emphasized the fact that we are different and beautiful."

"Amazing job! Good use of clothing items. Visual aids are always helpful!"

"I liked how enthusiastic and engaging Charmaine was. I think Charmaine did a fabulous job and loved everything about her presentation. Charmaine was so positive and has a great energy. I think she will be very successful and will encourage women to be more confident in themselves."

"Great visuals and clear presentations skills!"

"Thank you for the tips I will use them when I am next shopping for clothes."

Seminar Attendees

About the Author

Charmaine Bryan is founder of Charmaine Bryan Image Consulting. Charmaine coaches' individuals to improve their appearance, brand and communications skills. Through her signature packages Charmaine develops clients' confidence, credibility and visibility to take it to the next stage in their career. Charmaine also works with organizations that are looking for professional development programs and private coaching around appearance, behaviour and communication skills.

Charmaine consults on colour, style analysis, strategic wardrobe planning, closet audit, personal shopping, business, social and dinning etiquette and non-verbal communication skills.

Charmaine's seminars, workshops and lunch and learns will give you the know how to create your signature image. You will leave each seminar with many valuable tips and tricks that you can implement immediately. All presentations are customized to a group's particular needs and interests and guaranteed to be fun and interactive!

Charmaine is an Award-Winning speaker. She has achieved the Toastmasters Competent Communicator award. Charmaine delivers engaging speeches and presentations with a sense of humour. Charmaine currently serves as Vice President, Education at Project Management Toastmasters Club.

Charmaine earned her certification in Image Consulting through George Brown College. Charmaine is a member of the Association of Image Consultants International (AICI). Charmaine is a volunteer Stylist at Dress for Success Toronto.

Before becoming an Image Consultant, Charmaine worked in Education Administration for various government and not-for-profit organizations. Charmaine has a Masters in Policy Studies in Education and Bachelors in Sociology. Charmaine is also certified in Teaching Adults.

If you would like to book Charmaine for consultations, speaking or workshops contact her at info@charmainebryan.com, www.charmainebryan.com or www.stopbuyingclothesyou dontwear.com.

Foreword

Charmaine Bryan has mastered her signature style, and so can you. *Stop Buying Clothes You Don't Wear* will provide you with the correct training and the necessary tools to change your buying habits, just as Charmaine had. After reading this powerful book, I recommend it as a must read! Charmaine's brilliant mind will assist you with how you can save time and money to find your signature style for your professional and personal life. This book gives you step-by-step tips and strategies on how to dress for your body type and find your personal unique style. You will learn how you can build a wardrobe for your lifestyle, wear 100 percent of your wardrobe, and be a thrifty shopper if you are on a budget. In addition, Charmaine will show you what to look for when you are shopping.

Stop Buying Clothes You Don't Wear will give you a different approach before you spend money on a new outfit. You will learn how to "shop your closet" and use the gems that you already own to create mix and match ensembles to maximize your wardrobe. Throughout these pages, you will see the difference that these strategies have made to clients that Charmaine has worked with along the way.

You will never go shopping on a whim again, but will take into consideration what you already have hanging in your closet.

Raymond Aaron
New York Times Bestselling Author

Chapter 1

Journey To Your Signature Style

By opening this book, you have taken the first step to stop buying clothes you don't wear. You may have picked this book up because like most people, women especially, claim you have nothing to wear but yet have a wardrobe full of clothes. Not only do you have a lot of clothes, there are probably many clothes with the tags on that you bought on a whim or because it was on sale and seemed like a good buy at the time. You don't get around to wearing them because you do not like the fit, the colour, or it doesn't go with anything else in your wardrobe. The list could go on.

You are not alone I have been there myself. I used to have so many more clothes than I could ever imagine wearing. This was for various reasons, such as holding onto clothes that no longer fit believing I would get back into them some day, or buying things that were 50 percent off. What seemed like a bargain at the time was a waste of money when the clothes sat in the wardrobe with the tags on or I had no occasion to wear them. I love shopping in thrift and consignment stores, and again I fell into the trap because I would find great buys at rock bottom prices. When I discovered my love for clothing swaps the situation got out of hand as it was like getting clothes virtually free. I would pick up so many clothes, because it was a risk free way of trying another style that I would not usually go for. As the clothes were essentially free I would bring home bags of clothes. Sometimes even clothes that did not suit me, to bring them to the next clothing swap. Since becoming an Image Consultant, I learnt the tools of what looks great on me. I soon did away with so many of the clothes, shoes, and accessories that did not suit me or make me feel good. Now I have a wardrobe that is a quarter of the size it once was. I can say that I love everything in my wardrobe because I know it enhances me.

You are about to discover that by finding out what your signature style is you will spend less time and money buying clothes you don't need. Appearance is a tool to help you feel confident. If you look good you feel good! What you wear is a huge part of this. I know this personally, going from being very slender when I was younger to gaining weight over the years meant I could no longer wear the styles I used to. I wouldn't feel good about myself and would cover myself up in baggier clothes trying to hide my body. I didn't realize at the time doing that only made me look bigger. Someone looking at me could fill in the extra space. Once I learned to accept my body as it is now and dress for it accordingly I have found styles a lot more flattering for my shape. I no longer feel bad that I am not wearing that form fitting dress I used to go clubbing in my twenties. Instead I wear fabulous dresses that I always get complemented on.

The best part is you do not have to spend a fortune to look great. Many people have the impression that if you spend a lot of money on high fashion clothes you will look stylish. Unfortunately, if you are wearing something that does not complement your body type or style personality you are throwing away money on clothes and you still do not look and feel fabulous. You end up feeling uncomfortable and not wearing the clothes because you do not feel confident. Again, they sit in your wardrobe as clothes you don't wear.

Even if you feel you already have a polished look you can improve it. With this book, you will gain the tools and know how to have a wardrobe you love and wear everything in it. Before long you will see how applying a few of the strategies in this book will help you to do away with the frustration of feeling like you have nothing to wear. You will:

- Understand the specific outfits that work for you.
- Explore tips to help you look taller and thinner.
- Learn to dress appropriately for all occasions to appear confident and credible.
- Discover how to wear the right scale of accessories in proportion to your body.
- Master how to dress for your body silhouette and to look your absolute best in colours that will look great on you.
- Learn why you are only wearing 10 to 20 percent of your wardrobe.

- Evaluate your wardrobe to suit your lifestyle needs.
- Discover outfits you didn't know you had and create mix and match ensembles to maximize your wardrobe.
- Master having an outfit for every occasion ready.
- Understand how to shop your closet and spend less time and money in the stores.
- You will also gain tips on where to shop for the best deals even if you are on a tight budget.

I moved to Canada in summer 2012 from London, England. I only had one suitcase of Summer clothes. I needed to buy clothes for the Autumn and Winter and didn't have much money to spend on a brand new wardrobe. As mentioned before I started exploring thrift and consignment stores and found some brilliant clothing pieces for a fraction of the price. I always got complemented on the looks that I put together. Co workers were often amazed where I found my clothes. If you are on a budget, clothing swaps are another great alternative to build up your wardrobe as you are swapping what you already have rather than buying.

To get the most out of this book, I recommend that you read all the chapters first and go back to the chapters that apply to you and follow the tips in the chapters most relevant to your current situation. Every tip or strategy will move you one step closer to your goal of looking stylish with less. This in turn gives you more time, as you are not under pressure trying to decide what to wear every day.

I want you to read this book and take action. I want you to be ready to apply the strategies, tips and tactics within each chapter. Apply the many skills in this book and you will keep getting complements on your look. By using the knowledge in this book and taking action, I am confident that you will be as satisfied as the clients I work with who now stop buying clothes they don't wear.

Chapter 2

Develop Your Authentic Style Personality

The first step to finding your signature style is gaining an understanding of your style personality. Do you often wonder why some clothes are so you and others are not but work so well on others? We all have a unique style personality and it is the reason why some outfits work for you and others do not. In order to reflect your authentic self, you can use clothing and accessories to find your style personality. If you want to feel more like yourself, authentic, confident, comfortable and look great, wearing your personal style is the first step. You are not trying to become someone else you are not. Having your own style is key, so you know exactly who you are. It is important to be yourself through your clothing and wardrobe.

When you discover your unique personality style it will make sense. My client Hannah is tall and a plus size. The first thing she insisted that she did not wear dresses or skirts. She was more comfortable in trousers and leggings as she didn't like to show off her legs. What I discovered was she didn't like formal dresses. The environment she worked in allowed a smart casual look. Her features jumped out at me as being romantic. While we were shopping I selected some more feminine longer dresses for her to try on. She surprised herself and liked the fit of a black dress. She bought the dress that day. She said to me later that she felt confident and feminine whenever she wore it.

In order to gain the benefits of finding and wearing your own unique personal style involves four steps:

- Examine your personality, physical features and personal style.
- The seven personality styles.
- Fit your characteristics into your lifestyle and goals.
- Pull your personal style together.

Focus on your physical, personality, characteristics and personal style. You may be familiar with examining your personality or this process could be brand new to you. If so you will discover things you did not know about yourself.

Once you know what the different style types are, you will know what is related to each style. Some will resonate with you while others will not. Some styles involve straight lines, bold colours and simple design while others are curved, with soft colours and a complex design. Once you define your personal style it will become easier to shop as you will no longer waste time on styles that do not suit you and concentrate on what suits your personality.

Examine Your Personality, Physical and Personal Style Characteristics

Knowing your personality characteristics is important as they play a role in shaping your personal style. It is key to not just dive straight into the different style types as your personal and physical qualities are an important element of personal style.

Download the following lists of words from stopbuyingclothes youdontwear.com and circle the words that come to you first and best describe you.

Personal Style

Arty	Off Beat	Funky	Spicy
Classic	Town & Country	Soft	Tailored
Creative	Powerful	Executive	Sophisticated
Elegant	Refined	Traditional	Romantic
Gamin	Feminine	Supportive	Alluring
High Fashion	Trendy	Urban Chic	Striking
Sexy	Glamorous	Theatrical	Dramatic
Sporty	Natural	Casual	Athletic

Personality Characteristics

Energetic	Fun	Adventurous	Avant-garde
Unique	Contemplative	Comforting	Friendly
Authoritative	Credible	Delicate	Poised
Dynamic	Extreme	Relaxed	Skillful
Calm	Exciting	Carefree	Free-Spirit
Tender	Daring	Confident	Charming
Compassionate	Whimsical	Original	Gracious
Dedicated	Direct	Outgoing	Cute

The words you have circled will be useful when looking at style types, as they will shape your style personality. Keep these words on your phone or on your computer screen saver to remind you of them.

Create a Pinterest account that is a virtual scrapbook. You can create boards and pin things that are of interest to you. Your images may be of anything you are interested in destinations, properties, household furniture, sports, art, cars etc. Start now and keep pinning items. If you prefer you can create a physical scrapbook by cutting out pictures from magazines.

Next look at your physical features. Download from stopbuyingclothesyoudontwear.com and circle the word following each physical characteristic that best describes your personal attributes.

Height	Short	Average	Tall
Bone Structure	Fine	Medium	Strong
Facial Shape	Rounded	Oval	Angular
Hair Colour	Light	Medium	Dark
Hair Texture	Fine	Medium	Thick
Hair Lines	Straight	Wavy	Curly
Eyes	Large	Proportioned	Narrow
Eye Colour	Light	Medium	Dark
Body Type	Thin	Medium	Large
Body Line	Straight	Average	Curved

The Seven Personality Styles

The personality style system was developed by Alyce Parsons. The system consists of seven styles: Sporty, Traditional, Elegant, Feminine, Alluring, Creative and Dramatic.

The following charts will give you a brief overview of personality style. Read through all the charts clearly to see where your physical features and personality fit. There may be more than one that you fit into.

Style	Sporty	Traditional	Elegant
Fabric	Denim, cotton, natural fibres, slightly textured, crisp fabrics	Solids, fine woolens, jersey, natural blends and fabrics, crisp	Fine fabrics, cashmere, silk, smooth surface
Colour	Neutrals, bright colours, wears several colours at a time	Beige, navy, gray, blue, forest green, burgundy, wears two to three colours	Soft colours, subtle neutrals, often wears all one colour
Accessories	Small earrings, athletic shoes, backpack, sunglasses, baseball cap	Structured handbags, leather loafers, classic jewellery, cardigan	Fine classic pieces, pearls or semi-precious stones
Makeup	Natural	Natural, not overdone	Conservative
Hairstyle	Easy, carefree style	Neat and simple	Soft and sleek
Line	Tailored, relaxed, rounded lines	Tailored, straight lines	Classic lines, softly tailored
Design	More complex, lots of pockets, zippers, large buttons, allows for movement	Functional clothing, menswear detailing, timeless quality, moderate amount of detail	Minimal details, hidden zippers, buttons, impeccable fit and tailoring
Business attire	Suit worn with crisp blouse and sporty colourful accessories	Navy suit, soft coloured blouse classic leather shoes, belt and handbag worn with classic jewellery	Suit with graceful tailoring in soft neutral, may be skirt or trousers. Blouse in the same colour, or shade of the suit, fine, classic accessories
Messages	Fun, relaxed, energetic, athletic, friendly, cute, carefree, whimsical, playful, warm, animated, natural, outgoing	Credible, authoritative, skillful, confident, dedicated, reserved, composed, controlled	Elegant, confident, gracious, reserved, discerning, polished, dignified, cultivated

Style	Alluring	Dramatic	Feminine
Fabric	Knits, lycra, stretchy fabrics, smooth finishes, shiny, lightweight, tight leather	Firm fabrics that hold their shape, smooth fabrics, matte finish	Soft, flowing, smooth or slightly textured, lightweight, sheer
Colour	Black and white, red, hot pink, purple, emerald green, turquoise, wears solids or prints, animal prints	Black and white, red, purple, magenta, sapphire, emerald, bright and intense, high contrast colours	White, light gray, dusty blue, soft colours and pastels, wear all one colour or different values of one colour
Accessories	S-curved shapes, oval and curved jewellery, stiletto heels, strappy shoes and sandals, large hoop earrings	Bold statement accessories, designer sunglasses, oversized handbag that makes a statement, smooth finishes	Smaller, delicate detailing, sweaters with soft airy quality, delicate shoes and purse
Makeup	Smoky eyes and glossy lips, sultry makeup	Latest application, bold colours	Dewy, soft looking, soft play on eyes
Hairstyle	Full hair, tousled hairstyles	Very sleek and short, severe chignon	Long, soft curls
Line	Body hugging lines, s-curved lines	Slightly fitted to the body, exaggerated angles and shapes	Long, flowing lines, gentle-curved lines, soft details
Design	Minimal detail, form fitting, nothing classic in detail	Minimal detail, non classic, severely structured, sleek	Numerous details, rounded silhouette, no hard edges
Business attire	Black fitted suit with trousers or shorter straight skirt Bright coloured or appropriate animal print blouse	Black wool gabardine suit with asymmetrical closure	Soft neutral suit with curved details-skirt or trousers Light coloured blouse
Messages	Luscious, exciting, daring, spicy, sultry, flirtatious, enticing, bold, direct, flashy	Striking, dramatic, avant-garde, hip, dynamic, powerful, direct, sophisticated, bold, intense	Gracious, comforting, delicate, calm, tender, charming, compassionate, graceful, gentle, sensitive, caring

Style	Creative
Business attire	Suit with interesting styling or exaggerated silhouette, teamed with unexpected blouse or shell, interesting jewellery and shoes
Messages	Adventurous, artistic, unique, outrageous, unusual, imaginative, free spirited

Unlike other styles the creative style is not as straightforward, as creatives have a style or trend of their own which is more out there than other styles.

You will have identified one or two styles that best describe your personality style. How do they compare to your Pinterest board and the words in the first exercise? What physical features do you see in the styles that you identify with? Again, they may appear in more than one. Now you have identified your unique personal style. You will have a dominant style, a secondary or possibly a third style. This gives you the flexibility to wear different styles for different occasions.

Fit Your Characteristics into Your Lifestyle and Goals

You can use your different styles to find the balance between your personal and professional image. To do this you integrate your style knowledge with your lifestyle and goals. Identify where your personal styles fit into your lifestyle i.e. work, hobbies, sports, special events etc. Some styles are more suited to different careers. For example, female teachers may be seen as feminine. A lawyer may be viewed as traditional. Someone in advertising may have a dramatic or creative style. Where does your style fit into your personal life? The image you portray at work as a dramatic may not be the same image. In your personal life a feminine style may appeal to you. The trick is to incorporate some of another style but still be true to you.

If you worked in a corporate environment a traditional style would have worked for you. Now you are an entrepreneur, you may be looking for a creative look. With the different styles you can adapt them accordingly. You will only really discover your personal style by playing around with it. You may not get it right the first time. You can have fun with it, experimenting along the way.

Pull Your Personal Style Together

The best way to pull your looks together is to create a wardrobe formula for each of the styles, by using colours and accessories to soften or change looks. Use the tips below to develop your own wardrobe formula.

- Pick three styles that best work for you.
- Before going shopping look in your closet first. Keep items that belong to your styles and get rid of anything that does not (this will be discussed in-depth in chapter 6).
- Buy basics and core pieces such as jackets, trousers and skirts.
- When out shopping take, a prepared list of what you wish to buy so you don't buy anything on the whim.

You have completed the first step to finding your signature style for less. You have discovered what your style personality is and can now apply this when shopping for clothes. You will no longer waste time looking at styles that are not you. Next you will learn how to dress for body type.

Chapter 3

Mastering How To Dress For Your Body Type

In Chapter 2, I spoke about how your style personality can affect your signature style. Your body type also plays a key role in your style. My client Natasha would often go shopping and see something great on display and would try it on. She would do one of two things; buy it because she really liked it although she didn't like the fit much, or she would try it on and hate the item, but not understand why it looked so good on the display and looked awful on her. When I met with her, I could see she was wearing clothing that did not suit her body type. She was petit and would wear long dresses that made her look even shorter. After a style consultation with her she learned the tools to apply when thinking about what to buy. Since she was shorter I suggested she wear dresses that are short so that she can appear taller not shorter.

Knowing what clothing to wear to suit your body type is a huge advantage for you. You will stop buying clothes that do not suit your body type and therefore not have clothes you do not wear. You will also realise you do not need to beat yourself up about why something doesn't look good on you. It never was going to anyway because it was not made for your body type.

When dressing for your body type you have two options, to enhance or to camouflage. If you choose to enhance your figure you dress to your natural shape. If you decide to camouflage you dress to disguise the area you do not like and balance it out. You create detail and distraction elsewhere to hide it. For example, if you want an area to appear smaller you would wear deeper dark colours.

The following are key to dressing for your body type:

- Height
- Body silhouette
- Somatotype
- Facial shape
- Physical features and Personal texture

Dressing for Your Height, Body Silhouette and Somatotype

Height

If you are a woman under 5'4 or man under 5'9 you are short. Wear styles that are short, narrow and small. Have minimal details on clothing items. If you want details, wear them closer to your face. To appear taller wear details higher up your body. The length of the jacket is worn an inch above the top of your leg. The length of dresses and skirts is at the knee or shorter. Wear trousers that are narrow in leg and have a flat front. For tops the length is to the top of the hip or shorter.

If you are a woman over 5'6 or man over 5'11 you are tall. Wear styles that are larger, wider and longer. You can wear high contrasting colours. Details are larger and can be worn anywhere on your body. The Jacket length with skirts is at the top of your leg or longer. If you are wearing trousers, the jacket covers the derriere or worn longer. Jackets can be single or double breasted. For dresses and skirts the length is at the knee or longer. Trousers are wide leg, flat front or pleated. Top lengths are to the top of the hip or longer.

If you are a woman between 5'4 – 5'6 or man between 5'9 – 5'11 you wear clothes that are medium in length and size. You typically wear all one colour. Details are classic and medium. Jacket length with skirts is at the top of the leg. If you are wearing trousers, the jacket covers the derriere. It can be single breasted and flowing. Trousers are straight leg, flat front or minimal pleat. Dresses and skirts, length at the knee. Tops, length to top of the hip.

Body silhouette

There are six body silhouettes:

- Rectangle: Shoulders, hips and waist are symmetrical.
- Oval: Shoulders and hips are about the same size and waist tends to be wider.
- Hourglass: Shoulders and hips roughly same size, squared and waist is narrower. A desirable shape for women.
- Figure Eight: Shoulders and hips roughly same size and rounded and waist is narrower.
- Triangle: Shoulders are narrower than hips. Two types: waist is narrow like shoulders or waist is full like hips.
- Inverted Triangle: Shoulders are wider than hips and waist. A desirable shape for men.

Men are usually just the rectangle, oval, triangle and inverted triangle shapes. Go to stopbuyingclothesyoudontwear.com to view examples of body silhouettes.

You can identify your body silhouette by looking in a full length mirror. This is best done with fitted clothes on that outline your silhouette. First identify if you are long-waisted, short-waisted or proportionate. Place your hands at your natural waist. You are long waisted If your waist is closer to your toes than the top of your head. To create the illusion of length and balance, your trousers should be hemmed to the floor. You are short-waisted if your waist is closer to your head. To appear taller wear fitted tops or belts at the hip. Check the chart below to gain tips for your body silhouette.

Body Silhouettes	Tips for women	Tips for men
Triangle	Wide collars or horizontal lines at the shoulder area On the bottom, wear darker colors; wear body-skimming fabrics Straight-legged trousers, gored or trumpet skirts,	Jackets with vertical striping at shoulder or bulky details at shoulder Shirts should be untucked, structure at shoulder Tops with bulk at shoulder and should skim the body
Oval	Tops should be V-necks or wide scoop necks To add volume on the top wear military-style jackets, puff sleeves or flutter sleeves Dresses should have off the shoulder or sweetheart necklines.	Wear a top in one colour underneath a jacket to match Jackets with vertical striping at shoulder or bulky details at shoulder Tops with leather or suede at shoulder area with V or zipper front
Inverted Triangle	Wear fuller skirts or fuller-legged trousers to create the illusion of balance	Wear shirts tucked in Wear straight-legged trousers Wear a double-breasted blazer
Rectangle	Boat neck and scoop neck tops Sheath dresses or wrap dresses Trousers: straight or boot-cut to suggest curves	Wear a pin-striped suit if you are average height or shorter If you are tall avoid pin-striped suits
Hourglass	No balloon tops or dresses Nothing that hangs straight from your bust Use belts if you are not too short-waisted	
Figure Eight	Wear wrap style, V-necks or deep scoop tops Avoid anything hanging straight from bust Wrap style, fitted sheath dresses Stovepipe or straight-leg trousers	

Somatotype

Like body silhouettes understanding your somatotype is key to help you find your signature style. It was developed by William Sheldon; he describes three basic body types:

- Ectomorphs: tend to be straight, angular, lean or skeletal. Women tend to have a narrow bust or narrow hips. Men tend to have a narrow chest or narrow waist. Ectomorph's have linear features, straight hair, nose, mouth, flat.
- Mesomorphs: are average size and muscular. Women tend to have an average bust and average hips. Men tend to have an average chest or average waist.
- Endomorphs: are usually full body with a large bust or chest. Women may have a large bust or wide hips. Men may have a broad chest or wide waist.

You may overlap between the somatotypes. You could be a mix of Ecto/Mesomorph, Meso/Ectomorph, Meso/Endomorph or Endo/Mesomorph. Unlike your body silhouette that does not usually change, your Somatotype can change, due to diet and exercise.

The table on the next page gives some examples of what to look for deciding what to wear for your somatotype. If you fall between two take from both that relates to you.

Somatotype	Skirts and Trousers	Jackets and Tops	Patterns	Accessories and details
Ectomorph	Tailored, straight style, crisp fabric, pleats	Tailored, boxy style, crisp fabric, high neckline	Straight, stripe, check	Straight, angular styles, crisp, hard fabrics
Mesomorph	Classic, natural style, drape fabric, flat front or minimal pleats	Semi-fitted style, natural drape fabric, moderate neckline, classic style collar	Classic design	Classic, natural lines and shapes, minimal pleats or gathers
Endomorph	Soft, flowing style, draping fabric, longer skirts, Patterns, curved	Soft, fitted, draping fabric, low neckline, no collar or curved collar	Curved, floral, paisley	Curved, soft styles, draping fabrics, ruffles, gathers

What is Best for Your Facial Shape

The outline of the face can be straight or curved. Examples of straight faces can be diamond, v-triangle, a-triangle, rectangle and square. Curved faces can be heart, oblong, oval and round. To find out your facial shape pull your hair from the hairline. Check the outline of the face for curved vs. straight lines. Your face may be a combination of shapes. Go to stopbuyingclothesyourdontwear.com to see visual examples of facial shapes.

Facial shape	Necklines	Jewellery	Accessories and details
Rectangle	High neck, rectangular shape	Choker necklace, long narrow earrings	Rectangle toe in shoe, straight, small patterns
Square	Square, wide or deep or both, avoid high tight colours	Stud earrings, square, straight shapes	Square toe in shoe, square, check, plaid,
Diamond	Angled and narrow	Necklace reflects length and width of face, angular shapes	Angular/rectangle toe in shoe, hair classic style with straight edges
Triangle	V-neck, triangular or angular, notched collars, pleats	Dangling earrings, triangle and straight shapes	Triangle toe in shoe, patterns are angular, geometric
Heart	Sweetheart, V, curves, softness	Necklace reflects length and width of face, earrings, heart and curves shapes	Heart shape, soft triangle toe in shoe, curved and floral patterns
Oblong	Wide and shallow or high, oblong shapes	Choker necklace, long narrow medallion necklace,	Oblong toe in shoe, curved, small patterns
Oval	Moderate scoop, moderately close to neck	Pearls, oval shapes, moderate length earrings	Oval toe in shoe, patterns moderately curved
Round	Scoop, curved edges, wide or deep or both	Stud or hoop earrings, round shapes	Round toe in shoe, curved patterns, florals

Use Your Physical Features and Personal Textures

To determine your personal features, look for lines and shapes within your features and body to find out if they are straight, curved or balanced. If your physical features are straight you will wear straight lines, tailored, pleats, crisp fabric, straight patterns, stripe, check, plaid, etc. If you are curved you will wear curved lines, ruffles, gathers, draping flowing fabric, curved patterns, floral, paisley, dot, etc. If you are a balance of straight and curved wear classic lines. Avoid extremes of straight and curved, natural draping fabric, neither very soft nor very crisp, flexibility in pattern shapes.

Your personal texture can range from rough to smooth. A rough texture is curly hair and freckles. A smooth texture is smooth hair and smooth, clear complexion. Many people have a balanced texture. Generally, match your hair i.e. curly hair, texture, clothes and accessories. Straight hair, smooth clothing and accessories.

More Flattering Tips for Men and Women

- Women, to draw attention to the center of your body wear V-neck or scoop neck tops or dresses (depending on your facial shape being angular or round) with an eye catching necklace.
- Men, you should wear trousers to your natural waist, not too tight or too loose.
- If you do not want to look bigger then you should ideally wear clothes that fit closely to your body silhouette. Make sure they are not too big or too tight. If clothes are too big you are viewed as much as 10 pounds heavier than that what you weigh. If clothes are too tight, your body looks larger.
- Wear prints, patterns, accessories and details in proportion to your body. If you have a bigger frame do not wear delicate jewellery as it will get lost on you.

It takes time and dedication to learn to dress for your body. Accepting that everybody has a different shape and size and what looks good on your friend may not suit you due to different body dimensions. Once you master this you will always find clothes to flatter you. You will feel confident in your look and will find your signature style. If you do not have the time to do this consider hiring an image consultant who can help you get there in a shorter time. Taking the time to master this will reduce the likelihood of you buying clothes you don't wear. I will be discussing in the next chapter the importance of choosing the right colours for your wardrobe.

Chapter 4

Wear The Right Colours For You

Wearing your colours is another key step to finding your signature style. Do you have a dress or top that each time you wear it you feel great and you always get complemented on your look? On the other hand, you may wear something in another colour that washes you out. If you have wondered why some colours look great on you and not other people and vice versa there is a reason. It important that you wear the right colours for you. When you wear the wrong colours you see shadowing, it can make your face, hair and eyes look dull.

Here's what happens when you wear the right colours that complement your personal colour harmony. You look younger, more vibrant, healthy and thinner because you do not see the lines on the face. For women wearing the right colours is better than wearing the best foundation. The eye reads colour to make sure you are giving some life to your face. Your face is your communication centre, the colour reflects on your face and so that people look at your face and message instead of looking what you are wearing. Colour is a powerful tool. Colours can be energizing or calming to the wearer and the person looking at your colours. Colour can make you appear formal and powerful or friendly and approachable. The colours you choose to wear must work well with one another and with you.

There are only so many colours but what makes them different are the shades, tones and tints. You can wear the same colour as someone else but it could vary in the shade or tone. To know what colours are right for you, this is determined by your undertone. There are two types of undertone cool or blue and warm or yellow. If you look at the veins in your arms you can usually tell what undertone you are. If your veins are blue you tend to be cool and if they are green you tend to be warm. Your outer tone may change due to pregnancy, age, seasons, diet, or medication, your undertone never changes. If you are a cool undertone your colour season palette would be a summer or winter. If you are a warm undertone your season would be spring or autumn. Go to stopbuyingclothesyoudontwear.com for sample colours in each season.

Some Colour Terms

When describing colours there are a variety of terms that you can use:

- Pure colours are unmixed with other hues. Examples are green, red or magenta.
- A tint is lighter than the original colour, like ice cream flavours such as strawberry, pistachio and lemon sherbet.

- Shaded colours are a mixing result of an original colour to which black has been added. A shade is darker than the original colour. Think of a deep rich purple, navy blue or espresso brown.

- Muted or toned colours are a result of mixing a pure colour with any neutral/grayscale colour including the two extremes white and black. All tints and shades are also considered to be tones. Unless you have very dark skin or very fair skin and black hair, toned or muted colours will work best for you. Also toned colours tend to be more appropriate in a business setting. Raisin, paprika, moss green and French blue are examples of muted colours.

- Contrast is the relative lightness or darkness known to the value of adjacent colours. Examples are black and white, dark navy and pale yellow, or espresso brown and cream. Contrast can influence the image you are going for. If you want to show authority wear contrasting colours. Be careful when wearing these colours as the eye will be drawn to where the light and dark colours meet and if this is an area you would rather not draw attention to, wear clothes of a similar colour instead.

- Spring represents tint colours, summer are tone, autumn are tone and shade. Winter are tints and shade.

Wear Colours Appropriate for the Image and Function

You should keep in mind when choosing colours for the appropriate image and/or function. If you are looking for a:

- Professional and authoritative image wear neutral dark colours such as black, gray or navy.
- Professional, elegant and inviting image, wear light/warm neutral colours such as brown, taupe, tan, or camel.
- Light hearted open image in a casual outfit or sharp in a business shirt, wear light; white, cream or beige colours.
- More creative or comfortable image the colours are usually basic in green, blue, purple or burgundy.
- Fun, active, and outgoing image, the colours are accent red, orange, yellow, fuchsia, magenta.
- More sincere, honest and trustworthy image, or you work in sales wear a colour that is the same or similar to your eye colour. Wear a shirt or jacket in your eye colour near your face as you force others to look in your eyes that give them a feeling of trust.

Other Colour Tips

Many people use black as a neutral colour and will wear it with everything. Black does not suit everyone. If you have black or very dark brown hair, you probably look great in black. If your hair is lighter, it is less likely that black will look good on you. If you have a colour consultation you will find out your version of black alternatives that you can wear. These are very dark versions of your best colours and are usually dark enough to be worn with black belts and shoes. Examples of alternatives can be midnight blue, deep purple, very dark burgundy or maroon. If you wear black, or your black alternatives alone or with just a touch of colour, you send the message of stately elegance and authority which can come off as intimidating in black. That is great if that's your goal. If not consider another choice.

If you would like to look confident, dramatic, exciting, and powerful wear your version of red. Red is a great energy booster. However, if can make you tense If you're under a lot of stress.

If you have darker skin tones you look great in neutrals and are able to wear a wide range of colours. You can also wear some of the more intense hues.

Keep neutral colours to a minimum If you have red or blond hair and blue, green or hazel eyes. If you do wear neutrals add some colour with a blouse, scarf or colourful jewellery. You also look great when you wear colours in combination such as deep purple with a soft pink.

Many people think white is a neutral colour. White is brighter than the brightest colour and will stand out against other colours. It will make your teeth look yellow and the whites of your eyes dull. Wear your version of a white colour that matches both your teeth and white of your eyes.

Your Personal Colours

What trumps choosing colours for their impact or effect is wearing your personal colours. This is knowing your undertone and seasonal palette. If a particular colour or colour combination makes you look tired or older it overwhelms the look you are trying to achieve.

The best way to discover your undertone, season palette and wow colours would be to have a colour consultation with an image consultant. You will gain a more polished, vibrant and younger look. You'll learn what colours best suit your skin tone and that will make shopping for makeup, clothing and accessories easier and more cost effective.

My client Chantel come to me for a colour consultation because she wanted to find out what colours to wear to enhance her appearance through makeup, clothing and accessories. Through using colour flags, I first determined that Chantel had a cool undertone. From this I knew her season would either be a winter or summer. Comparing both the summer and winter colour flags Chantel looked brighter with winter colours. I also wanted to find Chantel's wow colours in her palate and they were red, purple and blue.

The next chapter will discuss how to access your lifestyle to dress for the right occasion.

Chapter 5

Dressing Appropriately For All Occasions

You now have a sense of your style personality, how to dress for your body type and what colours to choose. Another part in finding your signature style is knowing how to dress appropriately for all occasions. Once you figure out what occasions fit into your lifestyle you will develop a wardrobe that just fits this. Therefore, you will only keep or buy clothes for your lifestyle.

Nine Levels of Dressing

There are nine levels of dressing for a variety of lifestyle functions:

- Level 1 Business: Formal Corporate, are powerful and authoritative. You are a CEO, President, Lawyer, in high level Finance or any C level role.
- Level 2 Business: Corporate, are credible, reliable and flexible. You tend to work day to day in business.
- Level 3 Business Casual: Professional, are approachable and open. The field you are likely to work in is engineering, sales, politics.

- Level 4 Business Casual: Casual Professional, are creative and assessable. You tend to work in the teaching profession.
- Level 5 Casual: Smart Casual, are relaxed and friendly. You usually work in TV, advertising, marketing.
- Level 6 Casual: Active and Leisure, exercise, beach wear or lounging. You usually work in Fitness Instruction.
- Level 7 Evening: Informal, clubbing; casual date.
- Level 8 Evening: Semi-Formal, cocktail party; wedding.
- Level 9: Evening Formal, gala; ball; black-tie.

Business: Formal Corporate and Corporate

Formal Corporate

Suit	Colours are navy, charcoal, black, fabrics are fine wool; solid or pin stripe The style is classic, tailored, sharp, women wear skirt suits
Shirt	Colours are white, cream, fabrics are highly refined cotton The style is tailored, classic, men wear a shirt with a collar For women the neckline is to the base of neck
Tie	Colours are burgundy, blue, grey, fabrics are silk; solid, pin dot
Shoes	Oxfords for men, pumps for women
Jewellery	Gold or platinum; classic, understated, and professional

Corporate

Suit	Colours are dark or neutral, fabrics are fine wool; solid, pin stripe or subtle check The style is classic and sharply tailored; women wear skirt suits
Shirt	Colours are pastel or stripe, fabrics are highly refined cotton The style is classic; men wear a shirt with a collar For women the neckline is at least one inch from the base of neck
Tie	The colours match personal colouring; fabric is silk; may be stylized or abstract
Shoes	Oxfords for men, pumps for women
Jewellery	Gold or platinum; classic, understated, and professional One ring per hand, men, tie clip, women stud earrings

Business Casual: Professional and Casual Professional

Professional

Jacket, Trousers, Skirt	A jacket coordinated with trousers or skirt, or a suit in a non business style Fabric, texture and pattern can be stronger than corporate Colours can be lighter, softer, brighter and warmer
Shirt	Colours may be dark or bright, pastel or stripe Fabrics, small pattern may be woven or knit, cotton, silk or wool The style is classic; men wear a shirt with a collar. For women the neckline is 5cm from the base of neck
Tie	Fabric is silk; may be stylized or abstract if worn
Shoes	Men may wear loafers; women pump or trouser shoes
Jewellery	Neutral, metal, classic, may be modified to your personality
Casual Friday	You can wear this look for Formal Corporate casual Friday

Casual Professional

Sweater, Trousers, Skirt	Jacket/sweater and skirt/trousers, textures, colors, and patterns can be more distinctive and relaxed, fabrics may be tweed, corduroy, knits
Top	May be knit, men wear top with a collar. For women the neckline 7.5 cm from the base of the neck
Tie	Unusual pattern allowed if worn
Shoes	Leather and casual
Casual Friday	You can wear this look for Corporate casual Friday

Casual: Smart Casual and Active and Leisure

Smart Casual

Sweater, Trousers, Skirt	Jacket/sweater and skirt/trouser, may have medium to large patterns Fabrics can be suede, leather, denim, may include shorts, mini skirt
Top	May be chunky knits, T-shirts, (no slogan), sleeveless Women neckline at 10 cm from base of neck
Shoes	Sandals (not flip flops)
Belt	Match shoes leather metal, texture
Casual Friday	You can wear this look for Professional casual Friday

Active and Leisure

Bottoms	Light and bright, cotton knit, casual fabrics, jogging or exercise wear Short shorts, micro minis
Top	Tube, cropped, halter, tank, t-shirts with slogans, spaghetti straps
Shoes	Flip flops, athletic shoes

Evening: Informal, Semi-Formal and Evening Formal

Evening Formal

Women	Men
Gown is full-length	Black evening or tuxedo suit
Shoes and bag are evening style	White fine linen or cotton shirt
Jewellery is glittery	Black bow tie or regular
	Shoes, black evening slip-ons or lace-ups

Semi-Formal

Women	Men
Cocktail-length dress; sheer or shiny	Fine wool dark suit with a shirt in cotton or silk and dark silk tie
Shoes are shiny or match the outfit	Shoes are fine leather
Jewellery is glittery	
The look is sensual	

Informal

Clothing is sensual, but casual
Fabrics may have some evening detail, such as sheen

Accessing your Lifestyle

Having knowledge of what to wear for each occasion is key to prevent you from buying clothes you don't wear. To put this into action you need to conduct a lifestyle analysis. The aim is to identify current and projected life functions and the appropriate level of formality. Start by thinking about how you currently or anticipate spending your time. Round off the number of hours to the nearest 10 or 5 If it occurs less than once a week. Compare them to the levels discussed above.

Examples of functions you may do on a regular basis:

Presentations	Dating	Time with family	Training
Desk work	Relaxing	Meetings	Sports
Networking	Housework	Driving	Sightseeing
Reading	Shopping	Courses	Evenings

Once you have worked out how many hours you spend in each lifestyle you can go on to the next step of auditing your wardrobe to work towards having a wardrobe that matches your lifestyle. The end results in your signature style for less.

Chapter 6

Audit and Shop Your Wardrobe to Wear 100 Percent Of It

Why you Should Audit Your Wardrobe

In chapter 5 I introduced the nine levels of dressing and how to assess your lifestyle based on the levels. Now that you have done this it is time to audit your wardrobe. Why should you audit your wardrobe? A lot of people do not really know what is in their wardrobe and they claim to have nothing to wear but yet they have a wardrobe full of clothes. Most of us wear 20 percent of our clothes 80 percent of time. Therefore, almost 80 percent of the space in the wardrobe, is taken up by clothes we wear only 10 to 20 percent of the time.

Having a closet in chaos is a common challenge. Imagine this, you wake up in the morning and have a job interview but your wardrobe is a state and you have no idea what to wear. Or it is Saturday night and you have that all important date and they are due to arrive in 15 minutes. Do you want a solution which will mean you will not be in this situation again?

The answer to your problems are wardrobe modules. The key is knowing how to put outfits together that mix and match and not have a lot of single items or orphans that do not match with anything else and be left with nothing to wear. You conduct an audit to find out exactly what you have, what is worth keeping based on your lifestyle, your body type, your style personality, your colours and what is in fashion at the time.

Steps to Auditing Your Wardrobe

You should ideally audit your wardrobe twice a year. Spring/summer and autumn/winter.

Before you get started make sure you have:

- Dedicated time
- Bags for clothes you will donate
- A full-length mirror
- Hangers
- Plenty of space to hang clothes

Auditing your wardrobe will take hours the first time you do it, when it's done once it will be easier next time. You may want to ask a friend to help to cut down on time or hire an image consultant who is trained in a system to help you achieve it quicker.

The order of priority the wardrobe should be audited in is determined by assessing if your wardrobe matches your lifestyle. Start by laying out what is most important to you. For example, your business clothes for work as you wear them most of the time. Business clothes arranged in order, jackets level 1 and level 2, bottoms, shirts/tops, shoes, accessories. Level 3, jackets, bottoms, tops shoes accessories and so on until you continue through all the levels of formality as discussed in chapter 5.

Create a "Yes" pile, a "No" pile, and a "Maybe" pile of your clothes. Try on the clothes to see how they fit, look and feel. Only perfect-looking, well-fitting, current and classic clothes go into the "Yes" pile. In the "Maybe" pile, keep clothes you are uncertain about or that can be easily altered or repaired. You can show them to an expert or a friend to help you decide. In the "No" pile remove everything that:

- Does not fit, every piece of clothing in the wardrobe is for now, not for when you lose weight. If you insist on keeping clothes for future wear store them in another closet or area. Or get them altered to fit.
- Is worn out, you are giving the impression of a worn out image.
- Is outdated, if your look is outdated your skills may be perceived as such. Consider upcycling by getting them altered to a more up to date style.
- Does not feel great when worn. Any item that does not feel good is a compromise. This can come across when you are wearing it.

You end up with a lot of these clothes as you may buy something that is just okay for the occasion. You should feel great in all your clothes.

- Does not enhance the image. This is where you use what you have learned in previous chapters to ensure that your clothes support your body type and colouring, ensuring they fit how you would like, and the quality is appropriate for your lifestyle.

Once you have decided on the clothes that are in the "No" pile make sure you dispose of them straight away rather than having them laying around. You can sell them on e-bay, take them to a consignment store to sell (more details in chapter 9) or donate the clothes to a charity or thrift store. Next you will learn how to create wardrobe modules from the "Yes" and "Maybe" clothes.

What are Wardrobe Modules?

Wardrobe modules/capsule is a term coined by Susie Faux, the owner of a London boutique called "Wardrobe" in the 1970s. According to Faux, a capsule wardrobe is a collection of a few essential items of clothing that don't go out of fashion, such as skirts, trousers, and coats, which can then be mixed with seasonal pieces. This idea was popularised by American Designer Donna Karan, who, in 1985, released an influential capsule collection of seven interchangeable work-wear pieces.

You may ask why create wardrobe modules, and the main reason is that it saves time, money and space. According to the Bureau of Economic Analysis women will spend (on average) $3,400.00 per year on clothing. Yet we only wear 10 to 20 percent of what's in our closets. Wearing at best 20 percent of what we own, means we waste $2,700.00 per year buying clothing we don't wear.

The reasons for creating wardrobe modules:

- To have something for every occasion.
- Facilitate a put together look at all times.
- Gives an attitude of ease and confidence.
- Projects appropriate messages.
- Eliminates frustrating wardrobe shopping and costly mistakes.
- Allows you to have more time; be able to get dressed in ten minutes or less.
- Be able to create more options; mix and match your favorites.
- Accessorize better; no trouble finding matching pieces.
- Easily find your clothes in the closet because everything has its place.
- Look better and be a happier you.

Before you even think about heading out to the shops you need to create the modules so that you know exactly what is in your wardrobe and what you need to add to complete your modules. Otherwise you either have a wardrobe with a lot of individual items and nothing matches or you have multiple pairs of the same thing. For example, I used to have five pairs of similar black trousers.

Creating Wardrobe Modules Based on Your Lifestyle and Shopping Your Closet

Create a module of 20 hours for each lifestyle, for example; casual, smart casual, leisure, professional etc. Before building modules you need to decide how many hours you spend in each of the nine lifestyles so that you can put together modules that match this. For example, you may spend 40 hours in formal corporate, 20 hours in business casual, 25 hours in smart casual, five in evening wear, 10 in active and leisure. One module usually consists of eight outfits, one and a half modules 26 outfits and two modules 48 outfits. You can also mix and match clothes between the modules. Ensure that you have a module labelled for each function. Each module should fit your body type, lifestyle, personality style, colour and be in current fashion. Go to stopbuyingclothesyoudontwear.com for an example of a module. If you need modules for both cool and warm weather, ensure each module is labelled with the appropriate season.

- Select an outer layer such as jacket, cardigan or sweater.
- Find trousers, skirts or dresses that will work with the outer layer select a maximum of two.
- Select three or four tops that work with the outer layer and both bottoms. If one of them is a dress, you select one less top.

- For men, select up to two ties that will go with each shirt.
- Select shoes, belts and bags that work with tops, outer layer and bottoms.
- Select two pairs of hose/socks that match each bottom.
- Select jewellery and other accessories.
- Select appropriate underwear for this module e.g. a woman may need to ensure she has a t-shirt bra to have a smooth appearance under tops.
- Select an outerwear coat or jacket for this module.
- Ensure you write the descriptions of each item, colour, fabric, style etc. You may find it easier to take photos of the modules so you remember them exactly as they are.
- Write a list of what is needed to complete the modules for your next shopping trip. You do not need to commit to buying a full module, just half per season.

When selecting clothes and accessories for each module make sure that you are thinking about your personal colours and fabrics that are appropriate for the lifestyle. More neutral colours are ideal for work if it's a professional environment. Wear brighter colours such as greens, blues, purples for more casual work or social environments. Fabrics such as silk are only appropriate for evening wear and not during the day in the office.

Select design elements, scale, dimension, lines and shapes that match each other. Small patterns look better together than a small and large.

Fine jewellery should go with fine spaghetti strap tops. Pin stripes go with other pin stripes. Round circles with other circles. The texture of clothes should also be similar. If you are wearing a silk top, ensure the bottoms are also smooth.

Ensure that the pattern prints and solid colours go together as the solid colour picks up the colour of the print. For example, a black and white top may be worn with a white jacket and black shoes. When combining solids, use a maximum of three colours, secondary and accent colours appear two or three times. The dominant colour may appear more than three times. Like the example above keep darker colours lower (the black shoes) and lighter colours higher (the white jacket). Match belts and bags with your shoes, and may be lighter. The eye is usually attracted to the lighter or brighter colours first.

Joanne wanted a new look for a spring/summer wardrobe. She had also recently started a new job. Before her dress code for work was professional casual. The new job required her to dress more corporate and she wanted to make sure her work wardrobe reflected this. I asked Joanne to audit what she no longer wanted before we met. When we met I could see that with Joanne's current closet we could easily create over 50 modules. We prioritised the corporate clothes mixing and matching with skirts, trousers, jackets and shirts with accessories and shoes. We created two and half corporate modules. We created a further two smart casual modules as well as half a module for evening wear and another half module for active wear. We made a list of anything that was missing from each module. When we finished Joanne had some outfits as well as a shopping list of items she needed to buy to complete the modules.

If you follow these steps you will have a system where everything in your wardrobe matches, your clothes look great on you and more importantly you feel great and are no longer left wondering what to wear every day. In the next chapter I will discuss using accessories to extend your wardrobe.

Chapter 7

Extending Your Wardrobe With Accessories

Accessories are a great way of extending your wardrobe. Accessories can turn a simple look into a personal statement, especially with elaborate pieces. They are a fun and inexpensive way to refresh your wardrobe and express your creativity. The following are examples of accessories that you use to enhance or complete an outfit.

- Jewellery
- Scarves
- Shawls
- Capes
- Wraps
- Hats
- Watches
- Eyeglasses
- Belts
- Hosiery
- Shoes
- Bags
- Make up
- Nail polish

Why You Should Consider Wearing Accessories

You can use accessories to:

- Tie separates together. A blue and yellow chunky necklace would work with a yellow t-shirt and blue trousers.
- Show off your best features. If they are your eyes, wear some eye shadow with eyeliner and you will be getting complements.
- Reflect how you are feeling that day, or to vary your wardrobe to suit your mood. Wear sparkly earrings if you are upbeat. If you are feeling casual wear a hat.
- Break the ice at a social event, wear an elaborate accessory such as a pair of unusual earrings. This will provide a conversation piece.
- Add colour to your outfit that is predominantly neutral, add a scarf or a necklace in a complementary colour to draw attention to your face.
- Make your wardrobe more cost effective, you can extend it with accessories. In chapter 6 when you created wardrobe modules you added accessories. If you have a different set of accessories for different outfits each time you make a change, the cost per wearing of the dress or suit goes down because you have more ways to wear it.
- When you want to update an older garment add accessories. If you have a plain black dress you can team it up with an eye catching necklace, heels and a bracelet to match the necklace and

a clutch bag. You are ready for a night out without buying a new dress.

- If you want to wear two different colours that you would not usually put together. You could wear pink and gold and find a bag to match.

Know Your Body Type and Style Personality When Out Shopping for Accessories

You should match your accessories to your facial shape and texture. From chapter 3 you will have worked out if your face is angular or curved. Wear angled or curved accessories to follow suit. Use horizontal shapes if your face is long, and vertical shapes if your face is wide. If your skin is smooth and creamy, opt for smooth textured jewellery and scarves. Natural beads and scarves made of natural fibres usually look more harmonious next to skin with freckles or a rougher texture.

Wear accessories to match your body shape. Your accessories should carry the viewers gaze along a vertical line. Draw attention to your best features by placing an accessory where you want the viewer's eyes to rest. It is always best to place the most colour or design near your face to draw attention toward your face.

Bring out your hair colour by buying accessories in your hair colour. This can include a bag, a belt and several styles of shoes in your hair colour. If they are classic styles they go with everything in your wardrobe and can last for years. You can also consider beads, earrings and scarves that are in your hair colour.

Link your accessories to your style personality. In chapter 2 you will have found out your personal style. Each style has its own accessory personality. Some examples of accessories you could wear with each style.

Sporty: Fun and playful accessories

Earrings	Hoop or ball
Necklace	Pearl necklace or earthy pendent
Scarf	A short neckerchief worn around the neck, or ponytail
Shoes	Comfortable shoes
Bag	Practical handbags in natural materials

Traditional: Classic and toned down accessories

Earrings	Button
Necklace	Bead or pearl necklace
Scarf	A short neckerchief worn around the neck or on the handle of a handbag
Shoes	Closed toe, solid colour pumps or walking shoes
Bag	Shoulder bags in quality leather

Elegant: Smooth pared down coordinated accessories

Earrings	Match the necklaces
Necklace	Multiple strands of pearls, chains
Scarf	Elegant silk scarves
Shoes	Closed toe, solid colour pumps or walking shoes
Bag	Designer label bags of high quality leather and status materials

Feminine: Romantic accessories

Earrings	Small openwork or clustered
Necklace	Dainty, delicate necklaces
Scarf	Loose, flowing scarves
Belts	Soft leathers or fabrics tied as a sash or bow
Bag	Curved and unstructured bags in soft materials

Alluring: Seductive accessories

Earrings	Hoops or dangles with lots of movement
Necklace	Necklaces and pendants fit the cleavage of the bust
Scarf	Worn at the waist or hip
Belts	Wide, soft belts show off the waist
Shoes	Open designs with straps or low cut lines and high heels

Creative: Surprising, eclectic accessories

Earrings	Multiple earrings of different styles worn in one ear
Necklace	Unusual necklaces in a wide variety of materials often mixed together
Scarf	Large shawls draped across the shoulders or body, or tied at the hip
Bags	Medium to large fabric or soft leather bags or backpacks
Shoes	Low comfortable shoes or boots

Dramatic: Bold accessories that make a statement

Earrings	Oversized earrings
Necklace	Sculpted necklaces in quality metals
Scarf	Scarves in bold, contrasting colours worn asymmetrically on the body
Bags	Bags are structured and large
Shoes	Shoes are sleek and angular

How Your Bone Structure Relates to the Scale and Size of Accessories You Should Wear

To ensure you are wearing accessories to scale in details and choice of fabric you need to take into consideration your bone structure. If you have a:

- Fine bone structure, you have fine hair, a small face, narrow wrists and ankles and you are quite slender. Accessories should be fine, thin, flat, light-weight. Avoid large or overstuffed bags as you will not look in proportion.
- Strong bone structure. Thick hair, large face, wide wrist and ankles. Styles are strong, thick, chunky, and heavy weight. You can wear the large bag. Stay away from small pendants with delicate chains.
- Medium bone structure, you are between the two extremes of fine and strong. Styles are medium thickness and strength. Small size accessories will make you look larger and large accessories will look too big for you.

Tips On Shopping for Shoes

Shoes can either be great to shop for or they can be your worst nightmare especially when you are trying to find shoes to match an outfit for a special occasion. Here are some tips when purchasing shoes.

- Buy shoes later in the day as your feet will have spread and will not feel tight when you try shoes on. You want to make sure your shoes are comfortable.
- Like clothes shoes come in different styles. What may fit in one size in one style, may not be the same size in another. It can make a difference if you have a narrow or wide fit. My feet are wide so I know to not pick up narrow fitting shoes.
- Look for styles that suit your body type and personality. Look after your shoes by regularly polishing and brushing them so they will last longer.

The Accessory System

Karen Brunger developed a point system for assessing the degree of accessorizing. If you would like to find out where you fall on the accessory scale, follow the tips. Each accessory is worth 1 point. If the detail on the accessory is very elaborate, it counts as 2 points. The number of points can depend on fashion and whether the current look is simple or elaborate. If detail is very simple, then it receives 0 points

- 0-6 points is minimalist
- 7-12 points is classic
- 13-18 points is making a statement
- More than 18 is over the top

Depending on your style personality and the occasion you will want to be aiming for between 2-18 points.

Creating Modules for Your Accessories

As with your clothes you should have an audit and create modules for your accessories

- Sort through all your jewellery, belts, shoes, handbags and scarves.
- In the "No" pile remove anything you do not like, any broken pieces, colours or metal that do not complement you and jewellery not to your scale. Do not keep anything you cannot repair, hurt your feet, don't fit your personal style or body type or are not in fashion. Only include the scarves in your colours and take away what you do not like.
- In the "Yes" pile put the pieces together of similar colours and styles.
- To avoid keeping shoes and bags at the bottom of your wardrobe, store them inside your wardrobe on shelves or in a separate dresser. To protect handbags put them individually in old pillowcases or cloth bags.
- Create modules with your accessories. Put together jewellery, a scarf, shoes, belt and a bag in similar colours and think about them in relation to the wardrobe modules you created with your clothes. Take a picture of each module to remember what accessories go together.

Keep your accessories in a visual space (on a chest in your bedroom or in the walk in closet), so you remember to wear them and it becomes second nature to include accessories in your outfit. They can be organized in a jewellery armoire that will hold necklaces rings, bracelets, pendants and earrings.

When out shopping to buy outfits, you should always be keeping accessories in mind. If you do not have something to match the new outfit, buy something while you are out. There is nothing worse than getting home to find you have no accessories to go with the dress or suit you just bought. You only want to make the trip once, if possible. If you follow the above strategies, you can now use accessories to stretch your wardrobe. Colouring can affect your choices and being true to your personal style boosts your confidence. You can now put together accessory modules and love each item. You are nearly ready to step out into the world wearing your signature style with confidence. Next you will gain some tips when out shopping for what you need.

Chapter 8

Shopping Only For Clothes You Will Wear

Tips When You Are Out Shopping

In chapter 6, I said once you have identified what you need in your wardrobe, make a list before you go shopping.

Going shopping with a plan gives you focus. You can concentrate on what you need to buy rather than looking at items you do not need. If there is something you really like but it does not go with anything else in your wardrobe it is okay to still buy it. If you do be prepared to build a complete outfit around it. This is why you have a plan built around your wardrobe modules so you do not have to think about finding something for it later. If you do not buy a complete outfit at the time you will take the individual item home and it will stay in your closet with the tags on and you will forget about it. When you do eventually dig it out of your wardrobe you can no longer return it.

Only buy clothes that you love. If you love the outfit you will wear it. If you are only okay with it there is less chance you will wear it. Too many times people buy clothes because they need something for an occasion and settle on an item because they need something. This is why it is so important to plan for what you need to buy otherwise you may be forced to buy something last minute and not be thrilled with your purchase. You can experiment if you wish to try on something different. Once you decide you are paying for it you must love it. There is a wide selection of stores, brands and styles. If one store doesn't have what you like you can always go to another one. Just as long as you are leaving the store with a garment that fits you well and you love it. Make sure your wardrobe has plain basics that flatter your body and are comfortable.

Watch the price. Nobody loves a bargain more than I do when I go shopping, but do not let a bargain fool you into buying something you do not need and had no intension of buying. Again make sure you love the item and not because it is 70 percent off. Would you have bought the same item at the original price? Unless it is something you have had an eye on but could not afford it at the original price then you should buy it. If not, you should pass on it. If you do buy it but do not love it, you would have wasted money regardless of whether it was $100 off as you are not going to wear it. Buying something a bit more expensive is more value as you will wear it verses no value from the item that was half price and it sits in your wardrobe. It is better going home empty handed than buying something you are not happy about. Your objective is to love every price of clothing in your wardrobe. You will feel so much better about yourself and your wallet will also thank you.

Shop in stores that are within your budget. Look for the highest quality possible for the price range. Sales usually happen just before the next season starts or mid season. To keep in the loop of sales happening in your favorite stores get on their email lists, follow them on social media and subscribe to their website. You can also get to know the discount warehouses and stores that have good value.

To make sure you have the perfect fit always try clothes on in the store. Even if you are certain of your size. Every store has different sizes and you may be a 10 in one store but a 12 in another. Styles do not fit the same way. When you are in the store you have access to three way mirrors so that you can see what the outfit looks like from behind. An outfit may look great at the front angle but if you check the back it may not fit as well as you think. If you buy it without trying it on you may end up with an outfit you are only okay with. You have the hassle of taking it back to the shop. This takes more time than taking the time in the store to try it on and if it doesn't work you have saved yourself the journey back to the shop.

Accept that it is hard to find a perfect fit in trousers and it may take you a while to find a great fit. This means trying on many different pairs whether they are smart trousers for work or a pair of jeans. Both men and women have the same issue. Trousers are difficult to fit as they have to fit us in a lot of places. When I am shopping I am bringing in at least 10 pairs into the changing room with me. I am lucky to find one that fits just right. If you find trousers you really like but do not quite fit as well as you like, consider getting them altered.

To get good quality items look at the fabrics. The fabric should drape nicely. It should not be stiff or clingy. There should not be loose threads in the construction. Stitching be should be small and lie flat without any puckering. It is worth checking that garments pass the test and spend a little bit more as it means you are more likely to get more wear out of then than risking the item falling apart after one or two washes. To compare quality to price, try the following exercise. Go to a high end store in your city. When trying on clothes look for who is the designer or manufacturer, the price and the fabric. Look at the cut of the garment and feel the fabric. How does it fit and feel? Go to the least expensive clothing store and do the same thing. Compare both, it will give you an idea of what is good quality and what isn't.

Shopping is the perfect opportunity to make time for yourself. To get the most out of your shopping trip, go alone. You can concentrate on what you want and need, and it will be more productive. Shopping with others can distract you. It may take you time to find what you are looking for. You have to go into many different shops. If you go with others, they may not be as focused as you are. While it is nice to get a second opinion if you are trying something on, they may perceive the item as not your style or they are biased towards what they like and they may dissuade you. If you feel like you need a second opinion, consider hiring an image consultant to teach you how to shop and what your best choices are. You will also get tips on camouflaging areas you don't want to draw attention to, help you shop within your budget, your personal style, your wardrobe and lifestyle and find quality garments.

Make the effort to dress nicely when you go shopping as you will more likely get better service. Unfortunately, first impressions count if you want to be taken seriously even when shopping dress as you would in your everyday outfits. It is easier when trying outfits on when your hair is styled and make up is usually what it would look like. Wear clothes that are easy to remove. If they are a hassle to remove you will be less inclined to try clothes on.

Like grocery shopping do not go shopping for clothes hungry or thirsty. Make sure you are watered and fed as you will need the energy to keep going. Take a break in between if you need a drink or some food.

Tips on Fit when Shopping

Coat	Length for men, below the knee, for women, if full length, it covers the skirt
	Sleeve length, extends ½ inch longer than shirt sleeve
Jacket	If single- breasted, the bottom button is usually kept open. If double-breasted, the buttons are kept closed
	Collar lies flat against the back of the neck
	Shoulder edge is even with widest part of the arm
Trousers	Length for women, if narrow cut, they cover the anklebone, if regular cut, they fall to the shoe, if wide cut, they cover the instep
	Length for men, the hem rests on the front of the shoe with a slight break, and is tapered so that the back is ½ inch longer and touches the top of the sole
Shirt	Collar shows ½ = ¾ above jacket collar
	Shoulder seams sit at the edge of the shoulder on a classic set in sleeve
	Sleeve cuff shows about ¼ - ½ past jacket sleeve
Tie	Tip touches the top of the belt at its shortest, hangs ¼ inch below the belt buckle at its longest. The narrower end of the tie knot is a fraction shorter
Belt	The belt is worn comfortably when the middle hole is used
Bra	The fullest part of the bust is halfway between the shoulder and the waist
	There is no bulging or gaping, the back of the bra is horizontal

Don't Rule Out Getting Clothes Altered or Custom Made

The common assumption when you go shopping is that the clothes should fit you off the rack with no alterations. Men are more likely to get their clothes altered than women are. We tend to not want to wear the bigger size because the size you thought you wear doesn't fit. The focus should be on the fit not the size. Not all sizes are created equal as many manufacturers do not use the same models when fitting their clothes. Therefore, sizes will come up differently.

The best strategy is to buy clothes that fit the largest part of your body and take it in where it is smaller. If you have big hips and a small waist, buy trousers that fit your hips and get a tailor to take in the waist. Ask for recommendations for a tailor. Before getting anything altered be clear about what the tailor will do. Most alterations are straight forward. Sleeve length and trouser length, waist in or out.

Suits and dresses may not be easy to fit with ready-made clothes. If you find simple alterations are not enough you may want to consider custom or semi-custom. Custom made or Bespoke involves having a series of fittings to ensure the clothing is fit to your measurements. It is not possible to try on the style beforehand. Semi-custom, differs in that a model of the garment is tried on first. The item is cut from a standard pattern and altered to your measurements before it is assembled. More alterations can be made after the item is sewn. If you want to you choose the color, style, fabric, workmanship and fit, this is the most ideal option. Brides may go down this route rather than try to find a dress off the rack as they want a dress to be made especially for them on their special day.

Be aware that not all dressmaker and tailor's skills and attention to detail are the same. The quality of workmanship and fit can vary from being comparable to designer clothing to embarrassing errors. Make sure yours is at the top quality. The fees charged by dressmakers and tailors vary widely. Some carry their own fabrics, others do not. Getting a garment custom made does not mean it will be less expensive. Often the cost of having a garment made may be similar to purchasing a comparable garment off the rack. When purchasing fabric buy the highest affordable quality.

Following the above tips can help you become more focused when you are out shopping. You save money and get good value because you will only buy items that you need and like. Similarly, if you go down the custom made route you are getting clothes fitted exactly to your body measurements. The next chapter will cover thrift and consignment shopping if you are on a budget.

Chapter 9

Shopping Alternatives: Thrift and Consignment

In chapter 8 I gave you some tips on what to look for when out shopping. I realize you may be on a budget and cannot afford to buy a new wardrobe all at once, a situation I have been in myself on occasion. This is why I encourage you to buy half a module at a time so you are not investing too much in one go. In this chapter I will talk about some inexpensive ways to get a new wardrobe if you are on a budget. Shopping at thrift and consignment stores are some great alternatives to shopping in regular stores.

My client Tasnuva had a limited budget per month to spend on clothes. To get her budget to go further I introduced Tasnuva to thrift stores and clothing swaps. I encouraged her to get on the thrift stores mailing lists that often have 50 percent off sales. I also invited Tasnuva to a clothing swap where she bought a bag of clothes to swap that she was no longer wearing. At the swap she found a dress, jacket, and a few tops that suited her body type. The dress was a style she would not have bought. As it was a swap she felt like to could be more adventurous with her choices. She managed to get a few things for one of her modules at minimal cost.

What are Consignment and Thrift Stores

Most thrift stores are associated with a charity, and proceeds from sales of donated goods benefit that charity. The stock is donated; it can range from designer castoffs to past-season fast fashion. These stores can vary from well-lit, well-organized displays to daunting, dark, disorganized messes. Even if you've had a bad experience at one you should give them another try as you can find some hidden gems if you know what to look for.

Consignment stores tend to have better quality and newer goods compared to thrift stores. The items sold there have been brought in by sellers who receive a portion of the sale price, so store buyers tend to be picky about what they buy. Some specialize in designer goods only, but others are less choosy. This is a great option if you are looking to build a career wardrobe on a budget. Some consignment shops could easily be mistaken for high-end boutiques. If you are concerned about wearing used clothes or shoes, most consigned items have often been worn for fewer hours than department store floor models. In some cases, 20 to 30 percent of the goods have never been worn.

Consignment usually works in two different ways. Some consignments buy the items outright and offers 30 to 40 percent of the sale price, with the shop keeping the rest, although online consignment services now offer sellers a larger cut. Another option is where the shop sells goods for an owner. The owner keeps ownership of their item until it sells, if it sells. As the owner, you'd pay a small fee to the shop as compensation for them selling your item.

It's standard for you to drop off your items for a 30-, 60- or 90-day cycle. If your item doesn't sell within that period, some shops will discount the item (by say, 30 percent), or you will need to pick it up. You can expect to be charged a 25 to 60 percent commission, which the shop collects as its profit. Some shops offer you higher percentages if you take in-store credit instead of cash.

Online consignment outlets are more recent. These are great options if you want to buy used, but are looking for specific items. Since you can search for something specific from your own computer, you save time going from shop to shop and looking though the racks.

Etsy is great if you are looking for vendors specializing in used and vintage clothing, and unlike the online consignment outlets you can generally ask the seller specific questions about a garment or accessory. Most vendors list as vintage, but the term is used loosely and may include items that are only a couple of years old.

Thrifting or Consignment, What is the Better Option for You?

Thrifting may be the better second hand option when you're on a tight budget. Clothes in thrift shops tend to be less expensive than consignment shops. This doesn't mean you can't get bargains at consignment shops or that some thrift stores are not overpriced. But thrift stores are utilizing donations and trying to sell as many items as possible, while consignment stores are choosy about what they accept and must split profits with garment owners. Consignment shops will charge more.

If you are looking for casual items thrift stores are better. You can find office-appropriate and formal items at most thrift shops. However, thrift shops are more likely to accept a flawed item. People might choose to keep or consign fancy garments that are still in good shape, therefore you are more likely to find casual wear in thrift stores.

Thrift shops are good for if you are shopping for accessories. Scarves, bags and belts can be found at thrift stores for very reasonable prices. As they are small you are more likely to spot any damage or wear. You'll get better deals on good stuff if you thrift for accessories.

If you love the thrill of the hunt, thrifting is for you. Thrifting takes time and patience. If you love searching for amazing finds or breathtaking bargains, you will adore this type of shopping. If the process is as much fun as the finds you take home in the end, you're a born thriftier. I like nothing more than looking through a rack of clothes and finding some hidden gems for a fraction of the price that you would pay in a department store or boutique.

If you are a second hand shopping expert, you can hit the thrift racks with confidence and find those bargains. If you're new to second hand shopping, consignment shops might feel less overwhelming.

Consignment shops are best when you are looking for higher end labels and garments with less wear and tear. If you are looking for work clothing, consignment shops are generally stocked to the brim with work-appropriate garments in good shape. You'll spend more, but you'll get newer items for your investment. There are also fun casual items on the racks, too.

If you are looking for something specific consignment shops tend to have smaller inventories and are better organized than thrift stores, plus they stock classics pretty consistently. Now, if you're on the hunt for a red leather jacket with fringe and rhinestones, thrift stores or even eBay might be better bets. But if you're looking for button-front shirts, skinny jeans, colorful cardigans, or simple sandals and you aren't willing to hunt through multiple shops to find them, try consignment.

If you want updated versions most consignment shops only accept items that were made in the past three to four years, so you'll have an easier time finding current iterations of classic items. Thrift stores on the other hand will have classic items in abundance, and some will be exactly what you want. But they'll also have skirts from the 80s and blazers from the 90s, which may look just ever so slightly "off" to your eye.

If you tend to prefer mid-market and high-end clothes overall consignment is best. Thrift stores may stock them if you catch them after a mid range to high end donation but it is rare. If you love designer clothes but do not want to pay the prices, consignment shops can help you out.

If you are easing into second hand, if you get overwhelmed easily, are working on a tight timeline, or just don't enjoy the shopping process all that much, starting with consignment shops can make the transition to second hand shopping a bit smoother.

Tips When Selling To Consignment Stores

The item needs to be a recognizable brand name; most consignment stores are very brand-focused If you bring in a brand that their customer may not recognize it is less likely to sell. Mall/high street and designer items brands are always best.

Clothing and accessories should be in good shape. Consignment items needn't be 100 percent flawless, but they definitely need to be free of substantial damage. Rips, shredding, stains, damaged hardware or zippers, or anything that renders an item unwearable means it should be repurposed or possibly just thrown away. Do not bring them to thrift stores as they also cannot resell truly damaged goods.

The items should be contemporary. Some of the trendier, young, fashion-forward consignment shops will consider your vintage items, but many want modern clothes and accessories only. Most consignment stores are looking for clothes made within the past three to five years. The newer the better, in many cases.

If your clothes meet the above criteria do the following to help convince the store to buy them. Make sure they have been washed or dry-cleaned. Make sure accessories and shoes are also clean. Keep items wrinkle free by steaming or ironing every piece before attempting to sell. You want your stuff looking as new and fresh as possible.

Touch-up clothes so they are in tip top condition. Use the lint roller for any stubborn pet hairs or dry schmutz. Invest in a sweater shaver to deal with pilling. Trim or mend any stray threads, and make sure buttons and hardware are properly affixed.

Do your research and explore your options before you take your items to the nearest consignment store. As I said previously some will take your items, sell them, and pay you out afterwards. Others will evaluate your clothes beforehand and offer you cash or credit immediately.

Percentages will vary by shop and geographic location. Don't assume that larger or more well-known shops will give you better deals! Sometimes smaller outlets will give you a higher percentage of the sale. With online consignment services offering sellers 60 percent, if you're selling primo stuff, ask the local boutique for more than the minimum 30 percent cut. Avoid trying to sell before the Christmas holidays when sellers need cash and after when they're angling to offload unwanted gifts. Consider consigning your garments at a different time of year, when there is less competition.

Tips When Out Thrifting

The items you would buy when thrifting vs shopping in a department store may surprise you. At a thrift store you might be happy to pay a dollar for a pair of jeans with a small hole that could be easily repaired but you would not be prepared to do that for a brand new pair for $50. If you found a gently used designer jacket with a button missing in a thrift store but would not buy the same in a designer store for full price. You will learn what you are willing to compromise on when thrifting. There will also be deal-breakers that you wouldn't buy even if the price is rock bottom.

If there is body odour on clothes, it is not worth the hassle of trying to get the smell out of it. Stains are okay if you know you can remove it or you are going to upcycle the clothing and cut it up anyway. Visible stains on used clothing tend to be challenging to remove. If it is stained, it's possible that the person who donated it did so specifically because that stain proved stubborn to remove.

For missing buttons that cannot be replaced, simple generic buttons are easy to find in most fabric stores. Older and fancier blouses, coats, and skirts often feature buttons that you might spend a lifetime attempting to match. Before dismissing check to see if the spare button is stitched to the garment. If it is not there it is probably better to leave it rather than trying to hunt down a button you may not find. If you do decide to buy a garment with the above deal breakers tailoring or over-dyeing can mask or remove some stains, and swapping all the buttons on a buttoned garment often works. You have to decide how much time and energy are you willing to invest in this item to make it wearable. Would you be willing to do the same if the item were less expensive and/or brand new?

Best Time to go Thrifting

In this world of fast-fashion and consumer waste any time is usually a good time to go thrifting. To get the best out of your thrifting trips there are a few timing-related factors to consider. Towards the beginning of the season is the best time as you get access to the best donations. Most people clean out their closets at the start of the season to make room for new garments. Sure you can wait until garments have been marked down at least three times before buying. Thrift store items are so much cheaper than retail, even at full price. Waiting for markdowns will mean better bargains, but as the season begins to peter out, so do the seasonally appropriate offerings. Get shopping while the best items are available.

On the day the floor gets restocked, thrift stores are generally in a constant state of receiving, processing, marking, and selling donated goods. If you are not looking for anything season specific going in on refill day guarantees you the pick of the best stock. Find out from the staff when they put out their new stock.

On sale days, most thrift stores will offer 50 percent sales at certain times of year. In addition, most stores will do 50 percent off a certain color price tag once per week. Make sure you know when they are coming up. Again, ask staff for the dates.

Easing into Thrifting

If you are still not sure about thrifting, because of the disorganization, the lack of size selection/diversity, and the sheer amount of time it takes to wade through the racks at a used clothing store. You can ease into thrifting.

Consider the accessories. They are easier to look through, examine for quality and flaws, and assess for usefulness. Belts can be slipped on over whatever you're wearing. Scarves can be handled and experimented with in the aisles. Handbags can be tested out, filled with your own belongings, assessed for comfort. If you have a short time to visit a thrift store, accessories are an easy find.

Look at jewellery. Thrift stores are full of funky, cheap, unique costume jewellery. Again, if you do not have much time, you can quickly scan through jewellery. You look in the mirror and will know immediately if a necklace or pair of earrings will work.

Try on the coats as you do not need to go into the fitting room to do this. They are among the goods most likely to have aged well despite years of use, they are an incredible value when purchased used, and they are typically confined to a small section of the thrift store. Depending on their condition they may need dry cleaning before wearing.

Thrifting and consignment are a great way to extend your wardrobe especially if you are on a budget. I discovered that Toronto had some great thrift stores and I found some bargains that helped me build my autumn/winter wardrobe. I found items of clothing that still had tags on or had barely been worn. I found brands and designers that I wouldn't have dreamed of paying full price for. Needless to say because of the excellent value I was in the thrift and consignment stores on a regular basis. In the next chapter I will discuss clothing swaps, another cost effective way to build your wardrobe.

Chapter 10

Clothing Swaps

What are Clothing Swaps?

Clothing swaps are the most cost effective way to update your wardrobe. A clothing swap is a type of swap meet wherein participants exchange their valued but no longer used clothing for clothing they will use. Clothing swaps are considered not only a good way to declutter and refill one's wardrobe, but also are considered an act of environmentalism. The notion of swapping is not a new concept; however, many groups and organizations exist that hold clothing swaps, in a variety of sizes, to raise money and clothes for charitable donations.

Swishing refers to swapping an item or items of clothing or shoes or an accessory with friends or acquaintances. Parties must willingly give an item to participate in the transaction, once they have given an item they are free to choose something of interest from what others have offered. Value does not come into the equation, as swappers do not necessarily get an item of equal value and are free to choose anything that the other person if offering (without having to pay). It's a great opportunity for you to get rid of all those clothes cluttering up your wardrobe whilst reinventing your style at the same time - they do say one person's trash is another person's treasure, after all!

Clothing swaps originated in San Francisco, California with events hosted by Suzanne Agasi in the late nineties. Online clothes swapping has also become popular, with websites offering an environmentally friendly and frugal alternative to shopping.

Why Attend Clothing Swaps

On average, we throw away 30kg of unwanted items, per person each year. Not only is this damaging to the environment but it's damaging to our pockets as well! Instead of throwing all of these clothes away why not attend or even organise a clothing swap/swishing party?

Organising a clothing swap/swishing event doesn't have to be a lot of work, it can be as big or small as you want it to be. How about inviting some friends over with some drinks and nibbles and swapping your clothes that way? You could also hold an event at your local coffee morning, pr at a community centre, yard or garage sale. If you're feeling adventurous why not organise a larger scale event whilst raising money for charity at the same time?

What to Bring to Clothing Swaps

Swappable items include quality wardrobe items that you'd typically consign or donate. Items must be clean and in very good condition. Most swap-worthy items fall in 3 categories:

- New clothes, with tags
- Nearly new clothes, worn only once or twice
- Gently used clothing, worn, but still in very good condition

You should already have a bag of great give-aways ready when you audited your wardrobe. If not, please take a bit of time to purge your wardrobe prior to attending a clothing swap. Don't forget to go through your dresser, closets, armoire, under the bed, storage, etc. to try on and decide which pieces currently work with your lifestyle, body and personality.

Gather all the perfectly good wardrobe items that you no longer wear or use. Unused stuff clutters your life. Say bye with bliss, as you let go of items you no longer wear and make space for new-to-you pieces that you actually will wear.

Clothing Swap-friendly items:

- Coats
- Dresses
- Skirts
- Suits
- Trousers
- Jeans
- Tops
- Blouses
- Sweaters
- T-shirts
- Work-out wear
- Costumes
- Shoes
- Purses
- Jewellery
- Belts
- Hats
- Watches
- Bags

Styles may include:

- Classic
- Couture
- Designer
- Vintage
- Tailored
- Formal
- Elegant
- Eco-Friendly
- Hip
- Chic
- Sporty
- Trendy
- Street
- Rock star
- Funky
- Casual
- Preppy
- Romantic
- Tropical
- One-of-a-Kind
- Offbeat
- Whimsical

As with thrifting and consignment do not take any clothes that are ripped, dirty, stained items or those with broken zippers, etc. All items should be freshly laundered and/or dry cleaned. Most clothing swaps donate unclaimed items to various local non-profits that provide clothing to people in need.

Some Advantages of Clothing Swaps over Shopping

When trying on clothes in a store, things may be working against you. The price may be out of your budget, the size on the label is not your size, and there is the emotional frustration when things don't fit. It can make the store fitting room a stressful experience. When you attend a swap, however, you're surrounded by free clothes. Most people are at swaps to enjoy themselves and most of the time become a roomful of encouraging allies. When clothes arrive at the swap, they've been handled in many different ways. Sometimes they've been tossed in a dryer and shrunk. Or stretched out. Rather than depending on the number or letter on the label, you try something on that looks like it may fit.

Free is even better because you are not paying for the clothes. You are open to trying something different than you would in a store because the clothes are free. You can experiment more. When it's free, if it doesn't work, you bring it back to the next swap. Nothing lost, but perhaps a new style found. Do not go too crazy as you could end up with too many things you do not wear.

Getting rid of clothes can be difficult. We tend to keep items that don't fit because we hope we can squeeze into them again someday, or we're worried we'll gain weight in the future and end up needing them. We also paid good money for these items, and parting with clothing that is in perfectly good condition, even if we donate it to a good cause is challenging. Taking them to a swap may be more assuring knowing that they are going to a good home

Body sizes do not matter. If you are concerned there may not be anything in your size, do not fear. Swaps include everything from tops and bottoms to jewellery, purses, shoes, and other miscellaneous accessories and personal-care items, like shampoos and perfumes.

I really starting having a good time when I started going to clothing swaps. The best part was it was like getting a load of clothes for free, and this gave me the opportunity to experiment with styles I wouldn't usually. If they didn't work I hadn't paid for them and I could always bring them to the next swap. As I said because of thrifting, consignment stores and clothing swaps I managed to build up an extensive wardrobe. Co-workers would often say to me; you look great, is that another new outfit, you always look so well put together, you have a knack for putting together looks that suit you. This is why I am a huge advocate for wearing gently used clothes as you do not need to spend a ton of money to look great.

Chapter 11

Completing Your Signature Style

There you have it! The tips and strategies to find your signature style for less. The next step is to take action. Get started on your own by applying what you have learned in the pages of this book. Do not overwhelm yourself and do everything at once. Take it a step at the time.

If, however you do not have the time or need some coaching I provide a variety of packages. You can find the details in the about the author page and by visiting my website. If you do get in contact, let me know you read the book, and you will receive a free phone or skype discovery call.

My own experience of clearing out my wardrobe for one season involved five big bags of clothing and shoes to give away. Now I have a wardrobe where everything suits me, I am confident in what I am wearing and I have outfits for every occasion. If I do go shopping I only buy things that will complement other clothing in my modules. I want the same for you. Now go and get started!

www.ingramcontent.com/pod-product-compliance
Lightning Source LLC
Chambersburg PA
CBHW072207270326
41930CB00011B/2562